Champion
Billy Mills

by Lee S. Justice

 HOUGHTON MIFFLIN   BOSTON

THE PLACE: Tokyo, Japan
THE DATE: October 14, 1964
THE EVENT: The 10,000-meter race of the Olympic Games

Thirty-seven runners waited eagerly for the race to begin. Among them was Ron Clarke of Australia. Clarke held the world record in the 10,000-meter race. He had run it in just over 28 minutes. Ron Clarke was expected to win this race. But there were other champions in the group. The Russian gold-medal winner from the 1960 Olympics was here. Mohamed Gammoudi of Tunisia was another favorite. New Zealand had also sent a great runner.

Did the United States have a chance of winning a medal? No one thought so. American runners excelled in the shortest races, the sprints. No American had ever won the 10,000-meter race at the Olympics.

One of the American runners was wearing number 722. His name was Billy Mills. His fastest time was nearly a minute slower than Ron Clarke's record. A minute is a long time in a race. No one expected Billy Mills to finish among the top runners.

At the starter's signal, the runners were off! The pace was fast. After 8 1/2 minutes the leading group had already covered 3,000 meters. That group included the favorites. It also included Billy Mills.

Halfway through the race, Billy Mills was still with the leaders. He had beaten his own best time for 5,000 meters. But how could he keep up this burning speed?

One by one, the runners in the leading group fell back. The pace was just too fast for them. As the last lap began, three runners had pulled far ahead. They were Ron Clarke of Australia, Mohamed Gammoudi of Tunisia, and the athlete wearing USA 722. The spectators jumped to their feet and cheered.

Clarke was in the lead. Mills ran at his shoulder. Suddenly Clarke's elbow brushed against Mills. Mills almost lost his balance. He dropped back. Gammoudi saw his chance and pulled into first place.

The three runners headed into the last stretch of track. Mills picked up speed. The crowd roared with excitement. The American sportscaster's voice trembled as he said, "Mills is coming on!" Nearby, someone yelled, "LOOK AT MILLS! LOOK AT MILLS!"

With a burst of power, Mills dashed past Clarke, past Gammoudi, and through the tape. Mills crossed the finish line first!

"What a tremendous surprise here!" the sportscaster shouted. "Bill Mills of the United States wins the 10,000 meter!"

9

Billy Mills won the race, setting an Olympic record of 28 minutes, 24.4 seconds.

An Olympic official quickly came over to Mills to ask, "Who are you?"

Later, a reporter asked Ron Clarke if he had worried about Billy Mills. "Worried about him?" Clarke answered. "I never heard of him."

In sports, the term *upset* names a win that nobody expects. Billy Mills's run for the gold medal is still among the most famous upsets in Olympic history.

At the start of that 10,000-meter race, only one person believed that Billy Mills could win. That person was Billy Mills himself.

Billy Mills had grown up on the Pine Ridge Indian Reservation in South Dakota. He had learned valuable lessons from his Lakota family. A Lakota warrior was someone who deserved respect. A warrior was strong, brave, responsible, and giving. Billy's father had told him, "Live your life as a warrior."

To be a warrior meant to accept challenges. There were to be many challenges and obstacles in Billy Mills's life. Both of his parents had died by the time he was twelve. He felt terribly alone.

At first, Mills used running as a way to get away from his problems. One day, when he was feeling especially bad, he remembered his father's advice. Mills set a warrior's goal for himself. He would win an Olympic medal.

Mills won a track scholarship to the University of Kansas. After graduating, he joined the Marines and was on his way to his goal.

In 1964, when he won his gold medal, Billy Mills was 26 years old. At that time he was a lieutenant in the United States Marine Corps. He had trained for the Olympics with the All-Marine Track Team. Mills had been running 100 miles a week. And he had the competitive drive he needed to win.

"A warrior learns the power of giving," Billy Mills has said. Over the years, he has been generous in helping others. He has given his support to programs for Native Americans. Many young people have learned how to excel from the champion Billy Mills.